W9-BJG-391

MOONLIGHT

Harold Pinter was born in London in 1930.
He is married to Antonia Fraser.

ERRATUM
Page 1 line 1 should read:
I can't sleep. There's no moon. It's so dark. I

by the same author

plays

BETRAYAL
THE BIRTHDAY PARTY
THE CARETAKER
THE COLLECTION and THE LOVER
THE HOMECOMING
THE HOTHOUSE
LANDSCAPE and SILENCE
NO MAN'S LAND
OLD TIMES
ONE FOR THE ROAD
OTHER PLACES
(A Kind of Alaska, Victoria Station, Family Voices)
THE ROOM and THE DUMB WAITER
A SLIGHT ACHE and other plays
MOUNTAIN LANGUAGE
PARTY TIME

PLAYS ONE
(The Birthday Party, The Room, The Dumb Waiter,
A Slight Ache, The Hothouse, A Night Out,
The Black and White, The Examination)

PLAYS TWO
(The Caretaker, The Dwarfs, The Collection, The Lovers,
Night School, Trouble in the Works, The Black and White,
Request Stop, Last to Go, Special Offer)

PLAYS THREE
(The Homecoming, Tea Party, The Basement, Landscape,
Silence, Night, That's Your Trouble, That's All, Applicant,
Interview, Dialogue for Three, Tea Party (short story))

PLAYS FOUR
(Old Times, No Man's Land, Betrayal, Monologue,
One for the Road, Family Voices, A Kind of Alaska,
Victoria Station, Mountain Language)

screenplays

THE PROUST SCREENPLAY
THE SERVANT and other screenplays
(The Pumpkin Eater, The Quiller Memorandum, Accident,
The Go-Between)
THE FRENCH LIEUTENANT'S WOMAN and other screenplays
(The Last Tycoon, Langrishe, Go Down)
THE HEAT OF THE DAY
THE COMFORT OF STRANGERS and other screenplays
(Reunion, Turtle Diary, Victory)
THE TRIAL

poetry and prose

COLLECTED POEMS AND PROSE
THE DWARFS (a novel)
100 POEMS BY 100 POETS (an anthology)

HAROLD PINTER
Moonlight

faber and faber
LONDON · BOSTON

First published in Great Britain in 1993
by Faber and Faber Limited
3 Queen Square London WC1N 3AU

Photoset by Parker Typesetting Service, Leicester
Printed by Clays Ltd, St Ives plc

All rights reserved

© Harold Pinter, 1993

Harold Pinter is hereby identified as author of this work in
accordance with Section 77 of the Copyright, Designs and
Patents Act 1988.

All rights whatsoever in these plays are strictly reserved and
applications to perform them should be made in writing, before
rehearsals begin, to Judy Daish Associates,
83 Eastbourne Mews, London W2 6LQ.

*This book is sold subject to the condition that it shall not, by
way of trade or otherwise, be lent, resold, hired out or
otherwise circulated without the publisher's prior consent in
any form of binding or cover other than that in which it is
published and without a similar condition including this
condition being imposed on the subsequent purchaser.*

A CIP record of this book is available from the British
Library.

ISBN 0–571–17085–4 (cased)
0–571–17086–2 (pbk)

2 4 6 8 10 9 7 5 3 1

To Antonia
with my love

CHARACTERS

ANDY, a man in his fifties
BEL, a woman of fifty
JAKE, a man of twenty-eight
FRED, a man of twenty-seven
MARIA, a woman of fifty
RALPH, a man in his fifties
BRIDGET, a girl of sixteen

THREE MAIN PLAYING AREAS:

1. Andy's bedroom – well furnished.
2. Fred's bedroom – shabby.

(*These rooms are in different locations.*)

3. An area in which Bridget appears, through which Andy moves at night and where Jake, Fred and Bridget play their scene.

Moonlight was first performed at the Almeida Theatre, London, on 7 September 1993. The cast was as follows:

ANDY	Ian Holm
BEL	Anna Massey
JAKE	Douglas Hodge
FRED	Michael Sheen
MARIA	Jill Johnson
RALPH	Edward de Souza
BRIDGET	Claire Skinner
Director	David Leveaux
Designer	Bob Crowley

BRIDGET *in faint light*.

BRIDGET

I can't sleep. There's no moon. It's so dark, I think I'll go downstairs and walk about. I won't make a noise. I'll be very quiet. Nobody will hear me. It's so dark and I know everything is more silent when it's dark. But I don't want anyone to know I'm moving about in the night. I don't want to wake my father and mother. They're so tired. They have given so much of their life for me and for my brothers. All their life, in fact. All their energies and all their love. They need to sleep in peace and wake up rested. I must see that this happens. It is my task. Because I know that when they look at me they see that I am all they have left of their life.

Andy's bedroom.
ANDY *in bed.* BEL *sitting.*
She is doing embroidery.

ANDY

Where are the boys? Have you found them?

BEL

I'm trying.

ANDY

You've been trying for weeks. And failing. It's enough to make the cat laugh. Do we have a cat?

BEL

We do.

ANDY

Is it laughing?

BEL

Fit to bust.

ANDY

What at? Me, I suppose.

BEL

Why would your own dear cat laugh at you? That cat who was your own darling kitten when she was young and so were you, that cat

2

you have so dandled and patted and petted and loved, why should she, how could she, laugh at her master? It's not remotely credible.

ANDY

But she's laughing at someone?

BEL

She's laughing at me. At my ineptitude. At my failure to find the boys, at my failure to bring the boys to their father's deathbed.

ANDY

Well that's more like it. You are the proper target for a cat's derision. And how I loved you.

Pause.

What a wonderful woman you were. You had such a great heart. You still have, of course. I can hear it from here. Banging away.

Pause.

BEL

Do you feel anything? What do you feel? Do you feel hot? Or cold? Or both? What do you feel? Do you feel cold in your legs? Or hot? What about your fingers? What are they?

Are they cold? Or hot? Or neither cold nor hot?

ANDY

Is this a joke? My God, she's taking the piss out of me. My own wife. On my deathbed. She's as bad as that fucking cat.

BEL

Perhaps it's my convent school education but the term 'taking the piss' does leave me somewhat nonplussed.

ANDY

Nonplussed! You've never been nonplussed in the whole of your voracious, lascivious, libidinous life.

BEL

You may be dying but that doesn't mean you have to be *totally* ridiculous.

ANDY

Why am I dying, anyway? I've never harmed a soul. You don't die if you're good. You die if you're bad.

BEL

We girls were certainly aware of the verb 'to piss', oh yes, in the sixth form, certainly. I piss, you piss, she pisses, etcetera.

ANDY

We girls! Christ!

BEL

The term 'taking the piss', however, was not
known to us.

ANDY

It means mockery! It means to mock. It means
mockery! Mockery ! Mockery!

BEL

Really? How odd. Is there a rational
explanation to this?

ANDY

Rationality went down the drain donkey's
years ago and hasn't been seen since. All that
famous rationality of yours is swimming
about in waste disposal turdology. It's
burping and farting away in the cesspit for
ever and ever. That's destiny speaking,
sweetheart! That was always the destiny of
your famous rational intelligence, to choke to
death in sour cream and pigswill.

BEL

Oh do calm down, for goodness sake.

ANDY

Why? Why?

Pause.

What do you mean?

Fred's bedroom.
FRED *in bed.* JAKE *in to him.*

JAKE

Brother.

FRED

Brother.

JAKE *sits by the bed.*

JAKE

And how is my little brother?

FRED

Cheerful though gloomy. Uneasily poised.

JAKE

All will be well. And all manner of things shall
be well.

Pause.

FRED

What kind of holiday are you giving me this
year? Art or the beach?

JAKE

I would think a man of your calibre needs a
bit of both.

FRED

Or nothing of either.

JAKE

It's very important to keep your pecker up.

FRED

How far up?

JAKE

Well . . . for example . . . how high is a
Chinaman?

FRED

Quite.

JAKE

Exactly.

Pause.

FRED

You were writing poems when you were a
mere child, isn't that right?

JAKE

I was writing poems before I could read.

FRED

Listen. I happen to know that you were writing poems before you could speak.

JAKE

Listen! I was writing poems before I was born.

FRED

So you would say you were the real thing?

JAKE

The authentic article.

FRED

Never knowingly undersold.

JAKE

Precisely.

Silence.

FRED

Listen. I've been thinking about the whole caboodle. I'll tell you what we need. We need capital.

JAKE

I've got it.

FRED

You've got it?

JAKE

I've got it.

FRED

Where did you find it?

JAKE

Divine right.

FRED

Christ.

JAKE

Exactly.

FRED

You're joking.

JAKE

No, no, my father weighed it all up carefully the day I was born.

FRED

Oh, your father? Was he the one who was sleeping with your mother?

JAKE

He weighed it all up. He weighed up all the
pros and cons and then without further ado
he called a meeting. He called a meeting of the
trustees of his estate, you see, to discuss all
these pros and cons. My father was a very
thorough man. He invariably brought the
meetings in on time and under budget and he
always kept a weather eye open for
blasphemy, gluttony and buggery.

FRED

He was a truly critical force?

JAKE

He was not in it for pleasure or glory. Let me
make that quite clear. Applause came not his
way. Nor did he seek it. Gratitude came not
his way. Nor did he seek it. Masturbation
came not his way. Nor did he seek it. I'm
sorry – I meant approbation came not his
way –

FRED

Oh, didn't it really?

JAKE

Nor did he seek it.

Pause.

I'd like to apologise for what I can only describe as a lapse in concentration.

FRED

It can happen to anybody.

Pause.

JAKE

My father adhered strictly to the rule of law.

FRED

Which is not a very long way from the rule of thumb.

JAKE

Not as the crow flies, no.

FRED

But the trustees, I take it, could not, by any stretch of the imagination, be described as a particularly motley crew?

JAKE

Neither motley nor random. They were kept, however, under strict and implacable scrutiny. They were allowed to go to the lavatory just one and a half times a session. They evacuated to a timeclock.

FRED

And the motion was carried?

JAKE

The motion was carried, nine votes to four,
Jorrocks abstaining.

FRED

Not a pretty sight, by the sound of it.

JAKE

The vicar stood up. He said that it was a very
unusual thing, a truly rare and unusual thing,
for a man in the prime of his life to leave –
without codicil or reservation – his personal
fortune to his newborn son the very day of
that baby's birth – before the boy had had a
chance to say a few words or aspire to the
unknowable or cut for partners or cajole the
japonica or tickle his arse with a feather –

FRED

Whose arse?

JAKE

It was an act, went on the vicar, which, for
sheer undaunted farsightedness, unflinching
moral resolve, stern intellectual vision, classic
philosophical detachment, passionate
religious fervour, profound emotional
intensity, bloodtingling spiritual ardour,
spellbinding metaphysical chutzpah – stood
alone.

FRED

Tantamount to a backflip in the lotus
position.

JAKE

It was an act, went on the vicar, without a
vestige of lust but with any amount of
bucketfuls of lustre.

FRED

So the vicar was impressed?

JAKE

The only one of the trustees not impressed
was my Uncle Rufus.

FRED

Now you're telling me you had an uncle
called Rufus. Is that what you're telling me?

JAKE

Uncle Rufus was not impressed.

FRED

Why not? Do I know the answer? I think I do.
I think I do. Do I?

Pause.

JAKE

I think you do.

FRED

I think so too. I think I do.

JAKE

I think so too.

Pause.

FRED

The answer is that your father was just a little bit short of a few krugerrands.

JAKE

He'd run out of pesetas in a pretty spectacular fashion.

FRED

He had, only a few nights before, dropped a packet on the pier at Bognor Regis.

JAKE

Fishing for tiddlers.

FRED

His casino life had long been a lost horizon.

JAKE

The silver pail was empty.

FRED

As was the gold.

JAKE

Nary an emerald.

FRED

Nary a gem.

JAKE

Gemless in Wall Street —

FRED

To the bank with fuck-all.

JAKE

Yes — it must and will be said — the speech my
father gave at that trustees meeting on that
wonderfully soft summer morning in the
Cotswolds all those years ago was the speech
either of a mountebank — a child — a shyster —
a fool — a villain —

FRED

Or a saint.

MARIA *to them*. JAKE *stands*.

MARIA

Do you remember me? I was your mother's
best friend. You're both so tall. I remember
you when you were little boys. And Bridget of
course. I once took you all to the Zoo, with
your father. We had tea. Do you remember?

I used to come to tea, with your mother. We drank so much tea in those days! My three are all in terribly good form. Sarah's doing marvellously well and Lucien's thriving at the Consulate and as for Susannah, there's no stopping her. But don't you remember the word games we all used to play? Then we'd walk across the Common. That's where we met Ralph. He was refereeing a football match. He did it, oh I don't know, with such aplomb, such command. Your mother and I were so . . . impressed. He was always ahead of the game. He knew where the ball was going before it was kicked. Osmosis. I think that's the word. He's still as osmotic as anyone I've ever come across. Much more so, of course. Most people have no osmotic quality whatsoever. But of course in those days – I won't deny it – I had a great affection for your father. And so had your mother – for your father. Your father possessed little in the way of osmosis but nor did he hide his blushes under a barrel. I mean he wasn't a pretender, he didn't waste precious time. And how he danced. How he danced. One of the great waltzers. An elegance and grace long gone. A firmness and authority so seldom encountered. And he looked you directly in the eye. Unwavering. As he swirled you across the floor. A rare gift. But I was young in those days. So was your mother. Your mother was marvellously young and quickening every moment. I – I must say – particularly when I saw your mother being swirled across the floor by your father – felt buds breaking out all over the place. I thought I'd go mad.

Andy's room.
ANDY *and* BEL.

ANDY

I'll tell you something about me. I sweated over a hot desk all my working life and nobody ever found a flaw in my working procedures. Nobody ever uncovered the slightest hint of negligence or misdemeanour. Never. I was an inspiration to others. I inspired the young men and women down from here and down from there. I inspired them to put their shoulders to the wheel and their noses to the grindstone and to keep faith at all costs with the structure which after all ensured the ordered government of all our lives, which took perfect care of us, which held us to its bosom, as it were. I was a first class civil servant. I was admired and respected. I do not say I was loved. I didn't want to be loved. Love is an attribute no civil servant worth his salt would give house room to. It's redundant. An excrescence. No no, I'll tell you what I was. I was an envied and feared force in the temples of the just.

BEL

But you never swore in the office?

ANDY

I would never use obscene language in the office. Certainly not. I kept my obscene language for the home, where it belongs.

Pause.

Oh there's something I forgot to tell you. I bumped into Maria the other day, the day before I was stricken. She invited me back to her flat for a slice of plumduff. I said to her, If you have thighs prepare to bare them now.

BEL

Yes, you always entertained a healthy lust for her.

ANDY

A *healthy* lust? Do you think so?

BEL

And she for you.

ANDY

Has that been the whisper along the white sands of the blue Caribbean? I'm dying. Am I dying?

BEL

If you were dying you'd be dead.

ANDY

How do you work that out?

BEL

You'd be dead if you were dying.

ANDY

I sometimes think I'm married to a raving
lunatic! But I'm always prepared to look on
the sunny side of things. You mean I'll see
spring again? I'll see another spring? All the
paraphernalia of flowers?

BEL

What a lovely use of language. You know,
you've never used language in such a way
before. You've never said such a thing before.

ANDY

Oh so what? I've said other things, haven't I?
Plenty of other things. All my life. All my life
I've been saying plenty of other things.

BEL

Yes, it's quite true that all your life in all your
personal and social attachments the language
you employed was mainly coarse, crude,
vacuous, puerile, obscene and brutal to a

19

degree. Most people were ready to vomit after no more than ten minutes in your company. But this is not to say that beneath this vicious some would say demented exterior there did not exist a delicate even poetic sensibility, the sensibility of a young horse in the golden age, in the golden past of our forefathers.

Silence.

ANDY

Anyway, admit it. You always entertained a healthy lust for Maria yourself. And she for you. But let me make something quite clear. I was never jealous. I was not jealous then. Nor am I jealous now.

BEL

Why should you be jealous? She was your mistress. Throughout the early and lovely days of our marriage.

ANDY

She must have reminded me of you.

Pause.

The past is a mist.

Pause.

Once . . . I remember this . . . once . . . a woman walked towards me across a darkening room.

Pause.

BEL

That was me.

Pause.

ANDY

You?

Third area.
Faint light. BRIDGET.

BRIDGET

I am walking slowly in a dense jungle. But I'm not suffocating. I can breathe. That is because I can see the sky through the leaves.

Pause.

I'm surrounded by flowers. Hibiscus, oleander, bougainvillea, jacaranda. The turf under my feet is soft.

Pause.

I crossed so many fierce landscapes to get here. Thorns, stones, stinging nettles, barbed wire, skeletons of men and women in ditches. There was no hiding there. There was no yielding. There was no solace, no shelter.

Pause.

But here there is shelter. I can hide. I am hidden. The flowers surround me but they don't imprison me. I am free. Hidden but free. I'm a captive no longer. I'm lost no longer. No one can find me or see me. I can be seen only by eyes of the jungle, eyes in the leaves. But they don't want to harm me.

Pause.

There is a smell of burning. A velvet odour, very deep, an echo like a bell.

Pause.

No one in the world can find me.

Fred's bedroom.
FRED *and* JAKE, *sitting at a table.*

JAKE

What did you say your name was? I've made a note of it somewhere.

FRED

Macpherson.

JAKE

That's funny. I thought it was Gonzalez. I would be right in saying you were born in Tooting Common?

FRED

I came here at your urgent request. You wanted to consult me.

JAKE

Did I go that far?

FRED

When I say 'you' I don't of course mean you. I mean 'they'.

JAKE

You mean Kellaway.

FRED

Kellaway? I don't know Kellaway.

JAKE

You don't?

FRED

Yours was the name they gave me.

JAKE

What name was that?

FRED

Saunders.

JAKE

Oh quite.

FRED

They didn't mention Kellaway.

JAKE

When you say 'they' I take it you don't mean
'they'?

FRED

I mean a man called Sims.

JAKE

Jim Sims?

FRED

No.

JAKE

Well, if it isn't Jim Sims I can't imagine what Sims you can possibly be talking about.

FRED

That's no skin off my nose.

JAKE

I fervently hope you're right.

JAKE *examines papers*.

Oh by the way, Manning's popping in to see you in a few minutes.

FRED

Manning?

JAKE

Yes, just to say hello. He can't stay long. He's on his way to Huddersfield.

FRED

Manning?

JAKE

Huddersfield, yes.

FRED

I don't know any Manning.

JAKE

I know you don't. That's why he's popping
in to see you.

FRED

Now look here. I think this is getting a bit
out of court. First Kellaway, now Manning.
Two men I have not only never met but have
never even heard of. I'm going to have to
take this back to my people, I'm afraid. I'll
have to get a further briefing on this.

JAKE

Oh I'm terribly sorry – of course – you must
know Manning by his other name.

FRED

What's that?

JAKE

Rawlings.

FRED

I know Rawlings.

JAKE

I had no right to call him Manning.

FRED

Not if he's the Rawlings I know.

JAKE

He is the Rawlings you know.

FRED

Well, this quite clearly brings us straight
back to Kellaway. What's Kellaway's other
name?

JAKE

Saunders.

Pause.

FRED

But that's your name.

RALPH *to* JAKE *and* FRED.

RALPH

Were you keen on the game of soccer when
you were lads, you boys? Probably not.
Probably thinking of other things. Kissing
girls. Foreign literature. Snooker. I know the
form. I can tell by the complexion, I can tell
by the stance, I can tell by the way a man
holds himself whether he has an outdoor
disposition or not. Your father could never
be described as a natural athlete. Not by a
long chalk. The man was a thinker. Well,
there's a place in this world for thinking, I
certainly wouldn't argue with that. The

trouble with so much thinking, though, or with that which calls itself thinking, is that it's like farting Annie Laurie down a keyhole. A waste of your time and mine. What do you think this thinking is pretending to do? Eh? It's pretending to make things clear, you see, it's pretending to clarify things. But what's it really doing? Eh? What do you think? I'll tell you. It's confusing you, it's blinding you, it's sending the mind into a spin, it's making you dizzy, it's making you so dizzy that by the end of the day you don't know whether you're on your arse or your elbow, you don't know whether you're coming or going. I've always been a pretty vigorous man myself. I had a seafaring background. I was the captain of a lugger. The bosun's name was Ripper. But after years at sea I decided to give the Arts a chance generally. I had tried a bit of amateur refereeing but it didn't work out. But I had a natural talent for acting and I also played the piano and I could paint. But I should have been an architect. That's where the money is. It was your mother and father woke me up to poetry and art. They changed my life. And then of course I married my wife. A fine woman but demanding. She was looking for fibre and guts. Her eyes were black and appalling. I dropped dead at her feet. It was all go at that time. Love, football, the arts, the occasional pint. Mind you, I preferred a fruity white wine but you couldn't actually say that in those days.

Third area.
Jake (18), Fred (17), Bridget (14).
BRIDGET *and* FRED *on the floor.* JAKE *standing.*
A cassette playing.

FRED

Why can't I come?

JAKE

I've told you. There isn't room in the car.

BRIDGET

Oh take him with you.

JAKE

There's no room in the car. It's not my car. I'm just a passenger. I'm lucky to get a lift myself.

FRED

But if I can't come with you what am I going to do all night? I'll have to stay here with her.

BRIDGET

Oh God, I wish you'd take him with you. Otherwise I'll have to stay here with him.

29

JAKE

Well, you are related.

FRED

That's the trouble.

BRIDGET (*To* FRED)

You're related to him too.

FRED

Yes, but once I got to this gig I'd lose him. We wouldn't see each other again. He's merely a method of transport. Emotion or family allegiances don't come in to it.

BRIDGET

Oh well go with him then.

JAKE

I've told you, he can't. There isn't any room in the car. It's not my car! I haven't got a car.

FRED

That's what's so tragic about the whole business. If you had a car none of this would be taking place.

BRIDGET

Look, I don't want him to stay here with me, I can assure you, I actually want to be alone.

FRED

Greta Garbo! Are you going to be a film star when you grow up?

BRIDGET

Oh shut up. You know what I'm going to be.

FRED

What?

BRIDGET

A physiotherapist.

JAKE

She'll be a great physiotherapist.

FRED

She'll have to play very soothing music so that her patients won't notice their suffering.

BRIDGET

I did your neck the other day and you didn't complain.

FRED

That's true.

BRIDGET

You had a spasm and I released it.

FRED
That's true.

BRIDGET
You didn't complain then.

FRED
I'm not complaining now. I think you're wonderful. I know you're wonderful. And I know you'll make a wonderful physiotherapist. But I still want to get to this gig in Amersham. That doesn't mean I don't think you're wonderful.

BRIDGET
Oh go to Amersham, please! You don't think I need anyone to stay with me, do you? I'm not a child. Anyway, I'm reading this book.

JAKE
You don't want to be all on your own.

BRIDGET
I *do* want to be all on my own. I want to read this book.

FRED
I don't even have a book. I mean – I have books – but they're all absolutely unreadable.

JAKE

Well I'm off to Amersham.

FRED

What about me?

BRIDGET

Oh for God's sake take him with you to
Amersham or don't take him with you to
Amersham or shut up! Both of you!

Pause.

JAKE

Well I'm off to Amersham.

He goes. BRIDGET *and* FRED *sit still.*
Music plays.

Andy's room.
ANDY *and* BEL.

BEL

I'm giving you a mushroom omelette today
and a little green salad – and an apple.

ANDY

How kind you are. I'd be lost without you.
It's true. I'd flounder without you. I'd fall
apart. Well, I'm falling apart as it is – but if I
didn't have you I'd stand no chance.

BEL

You're not a bad man. You're just what we
used to call a loudmouth. You can't help it.
It's your nature. If you only kept your mouth
shut more of the time life with you might just
be tolerable.

ANDY

Allow me to kiss your hand. I owe you
everything.

He watches her embroider.

Oh, I've been meaning to ask you, what are
you making there? A winding sheet? Are you
going to wrap me up in it when I conk out?
You'd better get a move on. I'm going fast.

Pause.

Where are they?

Pause.

Two sons. Absent. Indifferent. Their father dying.

BEL

They were good boys. I've been thinking of how they used to help me with the washing up. And the drying. The clearing of the table, the washing-up, the drying. Do you remember?

ANDY

You mean in the twilight? The soft light falling through the kitchen window? The bell ringing for Evensong in the pub round the corner?

Pause.

They were bastards. Both of them. Always. Do you remember that time I asked Jake to clean out the broom cupboard? Well – I *told* him – I admit it – I didn't ask him – I told him that it was bloody filthy and that he hadn't lifted a little finger all week. Nor had the other one. Lazy idle layabouts. Anyway all I

did was to ask him – quite politely – to clean
out the bloody broom cupboard. His
defiance! Do you remember the way he
looked at me? His defiance!

Pause.

And look at them now! What are they now!
A sponging parasitical pair of ponces. Sucking
the tit of the state. Sucking the tit of the state!
And I bet you feed them a few weekly rupees
from your little money-box, don't you?
Because they always loved their loving
mother. They helped her with the washing-
up!

Pause.

I've got to stretch my legs. Go over the
Common, watch a game of football, rain or
shine. What was the name of that old chum of
mine? Used to referee amateur games every
weekend? On the Common? Charming bloke.
They treated him like shit. A subject of scorn.
No decision he ever made was adhered to or
respected. They shouted at him, they
screamed at him, they called him every kind
of prick. I used to watch in horror from the
touchline. I'll always remember his impotent
whistle. It blows down to me through the
ages, damp and forlorn. What was his name?

And now I'm dying and he's probably dead.

He's not dead.

Why not?

Pause.

What was his name?

Ralph.

Ralph? Ralph? Can that be possible?

Pause.

Well, even if his name was Ralph he was still the most sensitive and intelligent of men. My oldest friend. But pathologically idiosyncratic, if he was anything. He was reliable enough when he was sitting down but you never knew where you were with him when he was standing up, I mean when he was on the move, when you were walking down the street with him. He was a reticent man, you see. He said little but he was always thinking. And the trouble was – his stride would keep pace with his thoughts. If he was thinking slowly he'd walk as if he was wading through mud or crawling out of a pot of apricot jam. If he was thinking quickly he walked like greased lightning, you couldn't keep up with him, you were on your knees in the gutter while he was over the horizon in a flash. I always had a lot of sympathy for his sexual partner, whoever she may have been. I mean to say – one minute he'd be berserk – up to a thousand revolutions a second – and the next he'd be grinding to the most appalling and deadly halt. He was his own natural handbrake. Poor girl. There must be easier ways of making ends meet.

Pause.

Anyway, leaving him aside, if you don't mind, for a few minutes, where is Maria? Why isn't she here? I can't die without her.

BEL

Oh of course you can. And you will.

ANDY

But think of our past. We were all so close. Think of the months I betrayed you with her. How can she forget? Think of the wonder of it. I betrayed you with your own girlfriend, she betrayed you with your husband and she

38

betrayed her own husband – and me – with
you! She broke every record in sight! She was
a genius and a great fuck.

ANDY

BEL

She was a very charming and attractive
woman.

ANDY

Then why isn't she here? She loved me, not to
mention you. Why isn't she here to console
you in your grief.

BEL

She's probably forgotten you're dying. If she
ever remembered.

ANDY

What! What!

Pause.

I had her in our bedroom, by the way, once or
twice, on our bed. I was a man at the time.

Pause.

You probably had her in the same place, of
course. In our bedroom, on our bed.

BEL

I don't 'have' people.

ANDY

You've had me.

BEL

Oh you. Oh yes. I can still have you.

ANDY

What do you mean? Are you threatening me?
What do you have in mind? Assault? Are you
proposing to have me here and now? Without
further ado? Would it be out of order to
remind you that I'm on my deathbed? Or is
that a solecism? What's your plan, to kill me
in the act, like a praying mantis? How much
sexual juice does a corpse retain and for how
long, for Christ's sake? The truth is I'm
basically innocent. I know little of women.
But I've heard dread tales. Mainly from my
old mate, the referee. But they were probably
all fantasy and fabrication, bearing no
relation whatsoever to reality.

BEL

Oh, do you think so? Do you really think so?

Fred's room.
FRED *and* JAKE, *at the table.*

JAKE

The meeting is scheduled for 6.30. Bellamy in the chair. Pratt, Hawkeye, Belcher and Rausch, Horsfall attending. Lieutenant-Colonel Silvio D'Orangerie will speak off the record at 7.15 precisely.

FRED

But Horsfall *will* be attending?

JAKE

Oh, Horsfall's always steady on parade. Apart from that I've done the placement myself.

FRED

What are you, the permanent secretary?

JAKE

Indeed I am. Indeed I am.

FRED

Funny Hawkeye and Rausch being at the same table. Did you mention Bigsby?

JAKE

Why, did Hawkeye tangle with Rausch at Bromley? No, I didn't mention Bigsby.

FRED

They were daggers drawn at Eastbourne.

JAKE

What, during the Buckminster hierarchy?

FRED

Buckminster? I never mentioned Buckminster.

JAKE

You mentioned Bigsby.

FRED

You're not telling me that Bigsby is anything
to do with Buckminster? Or that Buckminster
and Bigsby —?

JAKE

I'm telling you nothing of the sort.
Buckminster and Bigsby are two quite
different people.

FRED

That's always been my firm conviction.

JAKE

Well, thank goodness we agree about
something.

FRED

I've never thought we were all that far apart.

JAKE

You mean where it matters most?

FRED

Quite. Tell me more about Belcher.

JAKE

Belcher? Who's Belcher? Oh, Belcher! Sorry. I thought for a moment you were confusing Belcher with Bellamy. Because of the B's. You follow me?

FRED

Any confusion that exists in that area rests entirely in you, old chap.

JAKE

That's a bit blunt, isn't it? Are you always so blunt? After all, I've got a steady job here, which is more than can be said for you.

FRED

Listen son. I've come a long way down here to attend a series of highly confidential meetings in which my participation is seen to be a central factor. I've come a very long way and the people I left to man the bloody fort made quite clear to me a number of their very weighty misgivings. But I insisted and here I am. I want to see Bellamy, I want to see Belcher, I need to see Rausch, Pratt is a prat

but Hawkeye is crucial. Frustrate any of this
and you'll regret it.

JAKE

I can only hope Lieutenant-Colonel Silvio
d'Orangerie won't find you as offensive as I
do. He's an incredibly violent person.

FRED

I know Silvio.

JAKE

Know him? What do you mean?

FRED

We were together in Torquay.

JAKE

Oh. I see.

Pause.

What about Horsfall?

FRED

Horsfall belongs to you.

Andy's room.
ANDY *and* BEL.

ANDY

Where is she? Of all the people in the world I
know she'd want to be with me now. Because
she I know remembers everything. How I
cuddled her and sang to her, how I kept her
nightmares from her, how she fell asleep in
my arms.

BEL

Please. Oh please.

Pause.

ANDY

Is she bringing my grandchildren to see me? Is
she? To catch their last look of me, to receive
my blessing?

BEL *sits frozen.*

Poor little buggers, their eyes so wide, so blue,
so black, poor tots, tiny totlets, poor little tiny
totlets, to lose their grandad at the height of
his powers, when he was about to stumble
upon new reserves of spiritual zest, when the
door was about to open on new ever-
widening and ever-lengthening horizons.

BEL

But darling, death will be your new horizon.

ANDY

What?

BEL

Death is your new horizon.

ANDY

That may be. That may be. But the big
question is, will I cross it as I die or after I'm
dead? Or perhaps I won't cross it at all.
Perhaps I'll just stay stuck in the middle of the
horizon. In which case, can I see over it? Can I
see to the other side? Or is the horizon endless?
And what's the weather like? Is it uncertain
with showers or sunny with fogpatches? Or
unceasing moonlight with no cloud? Or pitch
black for ever and ever? You may say you
haven't the faintest fucking idea and you
would be right. But personally I don't believe
it's going to be pitch black for ever because if
it's pitch black for ever what would have been
the point of going through all these enervating
charades in the first place? There must be a
loophole. The only trouble is, I can't find it. If
only I could find it I would crawl through it
and meet myself coming back. Like screaming
with fright at the sight of a stranger only to find
you're looking into a mirror.

Pause.

But what if I cross this horizon before my grandchildren get here? They won't know where I am. What will they say? Will you ever tell me? Will you ever tell me what they say? They'll cry or they won't, a sorrow too deep for tears, but they're only babies, what can they know about death?

BEL

Oh, the really little ones I think do know something about death, they know more about death than we do. We've forgotten death but they haven't forgotten it. They remember it. Because some of them, those who are really very young, remember the moment before their life began – it's not such a long time ago for them, you see – and the moment before their life began they were of course dead.

Pause.

ANDY

Really?

BEL

Of course.

Half-light over the whole stage.
Stillness. A telephone rings in Fred's room. It
rings six times. A click. Silence.
Blackout.

Third area.
Faint light. ANDY *moving about in the dark.*
He stubs his toe.

ANDY

Shit!

He moves to an alcove.

Why not? No fags, no fucks. Bollocks to the
lot of them. I'll have a slug anyway. Bollocks
to the lot of them and bugger them all.

*Sound of bottle opening. Pouring. He drinks,
sighs.*

Ah God. That's the ticket. Just the job.
Bollocks to the lot of them.

He pours again, drinks.
Growing moonlight finds BRIDGET *in back-
ground, standing still.*
ANDY *moves into the light and stops still,
listening.*
Silence.

Ah darling. Ah my darling.

BEL appears. She walks into moonlight. ANDY and BEL look at each other. They turn away from each other. They stand still, listening. BRIDGET remains still, in background.
Silence.
Lights fade on ANDY and BEL.
BRIDGET, standing in the moonlight.
Light fades.

Fred's room.
JAKE and FRED. FRED in bed.

JAKE

How's your water consumption these days?

FRED

I've given all that up.

JAKE

Really?

FRED

Oh yes. I've decided to eschew the path of purity and abstention and take up a proper theology. From now on it's the Michelin Guide and the Orient Express for me – that kind of thing.

JAKE

I once lived the life of Riley myself.

FRED

What was he like?

JAKE

I never met him personally. But I became a very very close friend of the woman he ran away with.

FRED

I bet she taught you a thing or two.

JAKE

She taught me nothing she hadn't learnt herself at the feet of the master.

FRED

Wasn't Riley known under his other hat as the Sheikh of Araby?

JAKE

That's him. His mother was one of the all-time-great belly dancers and his father was one of the last of the great village elders.

FRED

A marvellous people.

JAKE

A proud people too.

FRED

Watchful.

JAKE

Wary.

FRED

Touchy.

JAKE

Bristly.

FRED

Vengeful.

JAKE

Absolutely ferocious, to be quite frank.

FRED

Kick you in the balls as soon as look at you.

JAKE

But you know what made them the men they were?

FRED

What?

JAKE

They drank water. Sheer, cold, sparkling
mountain water.

FRED

And this made men of them?

JAKE

And Gods.

FRED

I'll have some then. I've always wanted to be a
God.

JAKE (*Pouring*)

Drink up.

FRED

Listen. Can I ask you a very personal
question? Do you think my nerve is going? Do
you think my nerve is on the blink?

JAKE

I'm going to need a second opinion.

FRED

We haven't had the first one yet.

JAKE

No, no, the second is always the one that
counts, any fool knows that. But I've got
another suggestion.

What's that?

What about a walk around the block?

Oh no, I'm much happier in bed. Staying in bed suits me. I'd be very unhappy to get out of bed and go out and meet strangers and all that kind of thing. I'd really much prefer to stay in my bed.

Pause.

Bridget would understand. I was her brother. She understood me. She always understood my feelings.

She understood me too.

Pause.

She understood me too.

Silence.

Listen. I've got a funny feeling my equilibrium is in tatters.

JAKE

Oh really? Well they can prove these things
scientifically now, you know. I beg you to
remember that.

FRED

Really?

JAKE

Oh yes. They've got things like light-meters
now.

FRED

Light-meters?

JAKE

Oh yes. They can test the quality of light
down to a fraction of a centimetre, even if it's
pitch dark.

FRED

They can find whatever light is left in the
dark?

JAKE

They can find it, yes. They can locate it. Then
they place it in a little box. They wrap it up
and tie a ribbon round it and you get it tax
free, as a reward for all your labour and faith
and all the concern and care for others you
have demonstrated so eloquently for so long.

FRED

And will it serve me as a light at the end of the
tunnel?

JAKE

It will serve you as a torch, as a flame. It will
serve you as your own personal light eternal.

FRED

Fantastic.

JAKE

This is what we can do for you.

FRED

Who?

JAKE

Society.

Pause.

FRED

Listen. I'd like – if you don't mind – to take
you back to the remarks you were making
earlier – about your father – and about your
inheritance – which was not perhaps quite
what it purported to be, which was not, shall
we say, exactly the bona fide gold-plated
testament deep-seated rumour had reckoned
but which was – in fact – according to

information we now possess – in the lowest
category of Ruritanian fantasy –

JAKE

Yes, but wait a minute! What exactly is being
said here about my Dad? What is being said?
What is this? What it demonstrably is not is a
dissertation upon the defeated or a lament for
the lost, is it? No, no, I'll tell you what it is. It
is an atrociously biased and illegitimate
onslaught on the weak and vertiginous. Do
you follow me? So what is this? I am entitled
to ask. What is being said? What is being said
here? What is it that is being said here – or
there – for that matter? I ask this question. In
other words, I am asking this question. What
finally is being said?

Pause.

All his life my father has been subjected to
hatred and vituperation. He has been from
time immemorial pursued and persecuted by a
malignant force which until this day has
remained shadowy, a force resisting definition
or classification. What is this force and what
is its bent? You will answer that question, not
I. You will, in the calm and ease which will
come to you, as assuredly it will, in due
course, before the last race is run, answer that
question, not I. I will say only this: I contend

that you subject to your scorn a man who was
– and here I pray for your understanding – an
innocent bystander to his own nausea. At the
age of three that man was already at the end
of his tether. No wonder he yearned to leave
to his loving son the legacy of all that was best
and most valuable of his life and death. He
loved me. And one day I shall love him. I shall
love him and be happy to pay the full price of
that love.

FRED

Which is the price of death.

JAKE

The price of death, yes.

FRED

Than which there is no greater price.

JAKE

Than which?

FRED

Than which.

Pause.

Death –

JAKE

Which is the price of love.

FRED

A great great price.

JAKE

A great and deadly price.

FRED

But strictly in accordance with the will of
God.

JAKE

And the laws of nature.

FRED

And common or garden astrological logic.

JAKE

It's the first axiom.

FRED

And the last.

JAKE

It may well be both tautologous and
contradictory.

FRED

But it nevertheless constitutes a watertight

philosophical proposition which will in the final reckoning be seen to be such.

JAKE

I believe that to be so, yes. I believe that to be the case and I'd like to raise a glass to all those we left behind, to all those who fell at the first and all consequent hurdles.

They raise glasses.

FRED

Raising.

JAKE

Raising.

They drink.

FRED

Let me say this. I knew your father.

JAKE

You did indeed.

FRED

I was close to him.

JAKE

You were indeed.

FRED

Closer to him than you were yourself perhaps.

JAKE

It could be argued so. You were indeed his youngest and most favoured son.

FRED

Precisely. And so let me say this. He was a man, take him for all in all, I shall not look upon his like again.

JAKE

You move me much.

Pause.

FRED

Some say of course that he was spiritually furtive, politically bankrupt, morally scabrous and intellectually abject.

Pause.

JAKE

They lie.

FRED

Certainly he liked a drink.

JAKE

And could be spasmodically rampant.

FRED

On my oath, there's many a maiden will attest
to that.

JAKE

He may have been poetically down trodden –

FRED

But while steeped in introversion he remained
proud and fiery.

JAKE

And still I called him Dad.

Pause.

FRED

What was he like in real life? Would you say?

JAKE

A leader of men.

Pause.

FRED

What was the celebrated nickname attached
to him by his friends with affection, awe and
admiration?

JAKE

The Incumbent. Be at the Black Horse tonight
7.30 sharp. The Incumbent'll be there in his
corner, buying a few pints for the lads.

FRED

They were behind him to a man.

JAKE

He knew his beer and possessed the classic
formula for dealing with troublemakers.

FRED

What was that?

JAKE

A butcher's hook.

Pause.

FRED

Tell me about your mother.

JAKE

Don't talk dirty to me.

Andy's room.
ANDY *and* BEL.

BEL

The first time Maria and I had lunch together
– in a restaurant – I asked her to order for me.
She wore grey. A grey dress. I said please
order for me, please, I'll have whatever you
decide, I'd much prefer that. And she took my
hand and squeezed it and smiled and ordered
for me.

ANDY

I saw her do it. I saw her, I heard her order for
you.

BEL

I said, I'll be really happy to have whatever
you decide.

ANDY

Fish. She decided on fish.

BEL

She asked about my girlhood.

ANDY

The bitch.

I spoke to her in a way I had never spoken to anyone before. I told her of my girlhood. I told her about running on the cliffs with my brothers, I ran so fast, up and down the heather, I was so out of breath, I had to stop, I fell down on the heather, bouncing, they fell down at my side, and all the wind. I told her about the wind and my brothers running after me on the clifftop and falling down at my side.

Pause.

I spoke to her in a way I had never spoken to anyone before. Sometimes it happens, doesn't it? You're speaking to someone and you suddenly find that you're another person.

ANDY

Who is?

BEL

You are.

Pause.

I don't mean you. I mean me.

ANDY

I witnessed all this, by the way.

BEL

Oh, were you there?

ANDY

I was spying on you both from a corner table, behind a vase of flowers and *The Brothers Karamazov*.

BEL

And then she said women had something men didn't have. They had certain qualities men simply didn't have. I wondered if she was talking about me. But then I realized of course she was talking about women in general. But then she looked at me and she said, You, for example. But I said to myself, Men can be beautiful too.

ANDY

I was there. I heard every word.

BEL

Not my thoughts.

ANDY

I heard your thoughts. I could hear your thoughts. You thought to yourself, Men can be beautiful too. But you didn't dare say it. But you did dare think it.

Pause.

Mind you, she thought the same. I know she did.

Pause.

She's the one we both should have married.

BEL
Oh no, I don't think so. I think I should have married your friend Ralph.

ANDY
Ralph? What, Ralph the referee?

BEL
Yes.

ANDY
But he was such a terrible referee! He was such a hopeless referee!

BEL
It wasn't the referee I loved.

ANDY
It was the man!

Pause.

Well, I'll be buggered. It's wonderful. Here I am dying and she tells me she loved a referee. I could puke.

Pause.

And how I loved you. I'll never forget the earliest and loveliest days of our marriage. You offered your body to me. Here you are, you said one day, here's my body. Oh thanks very much, I said, that's very decent of you, what do you want me to do with it? Do what you will, you said. This is going to need a bit of thought, I said. I tell you what, hold on to it for a couple of minutes, will you? Hold on to it while I call a copper.

BEL

Ralph had such beautiful manners and such a lovely singing voice. I've never understood why he didn't become a professional tenor. But I think all the travel involved in that kind of life was the problem. There was a story about an old mother, a bewildered aunt. Something that tugged at his heart. I never quite knew what to believe.

ANDY

No, no, you've got the wrong bloke. My Ralph was pedantic and scholastic. Never missed a day at night school. Big ears but little feet. Never smiled. One day though he did say something. He pulled me into a doorway. He whispered in my ear. Do you know what he said? He said men had something women simply didn't have. I asked him what it was. But of course there was no way he was going to answer that question. You know why? Because referees are not obliged to answer questions. Referees are the law. They are law in action. They have a whistle. They blow it. And that whistle is the articulation of God's justice.

MARIA *and* RALPH *to* ANDY *and* BEL.

MARIA
How wonderful you both look. It's been ages. We don't live up here anymore, of course.

RALPH
Got a place in the country.

MARIA
Years ago.

RALPH
Ten. Ten years ago.

MARIA
We've made friends with so many cows, haven't we, darling? Sarah's doing marvellously well and Lucien's thriving at the Consulate and as for Susannah, there's no stopping her. They all take after Ralph. Don't they darling? I mean physically. Mentally and

artistically they take after me. We have a
pretty rundown sort of quite large cottage.
Not exactly a chateau. A small lake.

RALPH

More of a pond.

MARIA

More of a lake, I'd say.

ANDY

So you've given up refereeing?

RALPH

Oh yes. I gave that up. And I've never
regretted it.

ANDY

You mean it didn't come from the heart?

RALPH

I wasn't born for it.

ANDY

Well, you were certainly no bloody good at it.

Pause.

RALPH

Tell me. I often think of the past. Do you?

ANDY

The past? What past? I don't remember any past. What kind of past did you have in mind?

RALPH

Walking down the Balls Pond Road, for example.

ANDY

I never went anywhere near the Balls Pond Road. I was a civil servant. I had no past. I remember no past. Nothing ever happened.

BEL

Yes it did.

MARIA

Oh it did. Yes it did. Lots of things happened.

RALPH

Yes, things happened. Things certainly happened. All sorts of things happened.

BEL

All sorts of things happened.

ANDY

Well, I don't remember any of these things. I remember none of these things.

MARIA

For instance, your children! Your lovely little
girl! Bridget! (*She laughs.*) Little girl! She
must be a mother by now.

Pause.

ANDY

I've got three beautiful grandchildren. (*To*
BEL) Haven't I?

Pause.

BEL

By the way, he's not well. Have you noticed?

RALPH

Who?

BEL

Him.

MARIA

I hadn't noticed.

RALPH

What's the trouble?

BEL

He's on the way out.

Pause.

> RALPH

Old Andy? Not a chance. He was always as fit as a fiddle. Constitution like an ox.

> MARIA

People like Andy never die. That's the wonderful thing about them.

> RALPH

He looks in the pink.

> MARIA

A bit peaky perhaps but in the pink. He'll be running along the towpath in next to no time. Take my word. Waltzing away in next to no time.

> RALPH

Before you can say Jack Robinson. Well, we must toddle.

RALPH *and* MARIA *out*.
BEL *goes to telephone, dials*.
Lights hold on her.

Lights up in Fred's room.
The phone rings. JAKE *picks it up.*

JAKE

Chinese laundry?

BEL

Your father is very ill.

JAKE

Chinese laundry?

Silence.

BEL

Your father is very ill.

JAKE

Can I pass you to my colleague?

FRED *takes the phone.*

FRED

Chinese laundry?

Pause.

BEL

It doesn't matter.

FRED

Oh my dear madam, absolutely everything
matters when it comes down to laundry.

BEL

No. It doesn't matter. It doesn't matter.

Silence.
JAKE *takes the phone, looks at it, puts it to his
ear.*
BEL *holds the phone.*
FRED *grabs the phone.*

FRED

If you have any serious complaint can we
refer you to our head office?

BEL

Do you do dry cleaning?

FRED *is still. He then passes the phone to*
JAKE.

JAKE

Hullo. Can I help you?

BEL

Do you do dry cleaning?

JAKE *is still.*
BEL *puts the phone down. Dialling tone.*

74

JAKE *replaces phone.*

> JAKE
> Of course we do dry cleaning! Of course we
> do dry cleaning! What kind of fucking
> laundry are you if you don't do dry cleaning?

Andy's room.
ANDY *and* BEL.

> ANDY
> Where are they? My grandchildren? The
> babies? My daughter?

Pause.

Are they waiting outside? Why do you keep
them waiting outside? Why can't they come
in? What are they waiting for?

Pause.

What's happening?

Pause.

What is happening?

> BEL
> Are you dying?

75

ANDY

Am I?

BEL

Don't you know?

ANDY

No. I don't know. I don't know how it feels.
How does it feel?

BEL

I don't know.

Pause.

ANDY

Why don't they come in? Are they frightened?
Tell them not to be frightened.

BEL

They're not here. They haven't come.

ANDY

Tell Bridget not to be frightened. Tell Bridget
I don't want her to be frightened.

Fred's room.
JAKE *and* FRED.
FRED *is out of bed. He wears shorts. They both walk around the room, hands behind backs.*

JAKE

Pity you weren't at d'Orangerie's memorial.

FRED

I'm afraid I was confined to my bed with a mortal disease.

JAKE

So I gather. Pity. It was a great do.

FRED

Was it?

JAKE

Oh yes. Everyone was there.

FRED

Really? Who?

JAKE

Oh . . . Denton, Alabaster, Tunnicliffe, Quinn.

FRED

Really?

JAKE

Oh yes. Kelly, Mortlake, Longman, Small.

FRED

Good Lord.

JAKE

Oh yes. Wetterby, White, Hotchkiss, De Groot . . . Blackhouse, Garland, Gupte, Tate.

FRED

Well, well!

JAKE

The whole gang. Donovan, Ironside, Wallace, McCool . . . Ottuna, Muggeridge, Carpentier, Finn.

FRED

Speeches?

JAKE

Very moving.

FRED

Who spoke?

JAKE

Oh . . . Hazeldine, McCormick, Bugatti, Black, Forrester, Galloway, Springfield, Gaunt.

FRED

He was much loved.

JAKE

Well, you loved him yourself, didn't you?

FRED

I loved him. I loved him like a father.

Third area.

BRIDGET

Once someone said to me – I think it was my mother or my father – anyway, they said to me – We've been invited to a party. You've been invited too. But you'll have to come by yourself, alone. You won't have to dress up. You just have to wait until the moon is down.

Pause.

They told me where the party was. It was in a house at the end of a lane. But they told me the party wouldn't begin until the moon had gone down.

Pause.

I got dressed in something old and I waited for the moon to go down. I waited a long

79

time. Then I set out for the house. The moon was bright and quite still.

Pause.

When I got to the house it was bathed in moonlight. The house, the glade, the lane, were all bathed in moonlight. But the inside of the house was dark and all the windows were dark. There was no sound.

Pause.

I stood there in the moonlight and waited for the moon to go down.